A New True Book

THE METRIC SYSTEM

By Allan Fowler

CHILDRENS PRESS ®
CHICAGO

A Canadian highway sign
shows both metric and
customary distances.

PHOTO CREDITS
AP/Wide World Photos–43
The Bettmann Archive–17, 20, 21, 24
© Reinhard Brucker–Milwaukee Public Museum,
18; 27 (left), 28 (inset)
© Cameramann International, Ltd.–10, 37
Odyssey/Frerck/Chicago–© Robert Frerck, 4, 11
Chip and Rosa Maria de la Cueva Peterson–7
PhotoEdit–© Richard Hutchings, Cover, 35;
© Elizabeth Zuckerman, 15; © David Young-Wolff,
16, 27 (right); © Myrleen Ferguson Cate, 45
(right)
Photri–© A. Novak, 12; © Brian Drake, 30
Reuters/Bettmann–28
Tom Stack & Associates–© John Cancalosi,
Cover Inset
Tony Stone Images–© Paul Damien, 23
SuperStock International, Inc.–© Tom Rosenthal,
40
Unicorn Stock Photos–© Karen Holsinger Mullen,
2, 45 (left); © Aneal Vohra, 8; © Tom McCarthy,
38; © Martha McBride, 39 (left); © Dede Gilman,
39 (right);
UPI/Bettmann–32
COVER: Boy being weighed on a metric scale
COVER INSET: Sign in Australia–Wombat
crossing

Project Editor: Fran Dyra
Design: Margrit Fiddle
Photo Research: Feldman & Associates, Inc.

Library of Congress Cataloging-in-Publication Data

Fowler, Allan.
   The metric system / by Allan Fowler.
      p.   cm.–(A New true book)
   Includes index.
   ISBN 0-516-01076-X
   1.   Metric system–Juvenile literature.
[1.   Metric system.]   I.   Title.
QC92.5.F68 1995   94-36352
530.8'12–dc20   CIP
                                        AC

TABLE OF CONTENTS

In this market in Barcelona, Spain, fruits and vegetables are weighed in metric grams and kilograms.

INTRODUCTION

Everywhere in the world people use a very simple system to measure things— the metric system.

Everywhere, that is, except the United States.

Is the metric system easy to learn? Yes! If you can multiply by ten and divide by ten, you already know how to work with metric. After all those arithmetic problems you've done—converting feet to miles or ounces to pounds—the metric system will be a breeze!

So go metric today—with the rest of the world.

A WORLDWIDE SYSTEM

Imagine you are visiting a country outside the United States—say Canada or France, for example. You look out the window of your hotel room one morning. The day is bright and sunny—but is it warm or cold?

You turn on the TV set and a weather reporter announces the temperature—27 degrees. Sounds pretty cold, doesn't it?

A French TV weather reporter with a map of
France that shows Celsius temperatures

But you know the
country you're visiting uses
the metric system for all or
most of its measurements.
And 27 degrees in the
metric system (or 27
degrees Celsius) is about
the same as 80 degrees

under the system we use in the United States (or 80 degrees Fahrenheit). You don't even need a jacket.

In Canada, highway signs show metric distances. "Speed limit 100" means 100 kilometers per hour– not 100 miles per hour!

This Canadian highway sign gives the speed limit as 100 kilometers or 62 miles per hour.

The United States is the only major country in the world that doesn't use the metric system. Our system is known as the English, or customary, system. While we measure distances in inches, feet, and miles, the rest of the world measures in centimeters, meters, and kilometers.

When you've been thinking in terms of pounds, pints, feet, and Fahrenheit all your life, it

You may not be able to read Japanese, but if you know metric you can tell what the temperature is from this sign in Tokyo, Japan.

might seem unnecessary to learn the metric system. But you will need to know metric, not only if you travel to other countries, but also if you work for a company that does business with other countries.

You will need to know the metric system when you study science. You'll use it every day if you work in a technical field. And you will need to know metric just to keep

Scientists all over the world use the metric system in their work. These biologists in Hawaii are experimenting with plants.

Billboards like this one help people learn the metric system.

up with things because the United States is "going metric" in more and more ways.

The good news is that the metric system is much easier to learn and use than the system you're using now.

SIMPLE AND LOGICAL

Our old nonmetric system requires lots of arithmetic. To change inches into feet, you must divide by 12. To change feet into miles, you must divide by 5,280. An ounce is $1/16$ of a pound. An acre equals 43,560 square feet.

And the point where water freezes into ice is not 0 degrees on the

Fahrenheit thermometer, as you might expect, but 32 degrees.

When you learned multiplication, the 10 times table was very likely your favorite. To multiply any number by 10, you just add a zero. Add another zero and you've multiplied it by 100. To divide a number by 10, just drop in a decimal point. For example, 893,276 divided by 10 is 89,327.6.

The decimal point is one

With the customary system of measurement, you have to do lots of arithmetic. The metric system is easier!

of the most useful ideas anyone ever came up with. It lets you multiply or divide by 10, 100, 1,000, and so on, merely by moving a little dot left or right.

Now, instead of a random bunch of numbers like 16 or 5,280 or 43,560, wouldn't it be great if all

With the customary system, you often have to add up fractions of inches like 10 3/4 and 8 3/8. The metric system is easier!

weights and measures and temperatures were in multiples of 10? Well, in the metric system, they are! That's why the metric system is so much easier to work with than the system that most Americans still use in daily life. You could say that metric is ten times easier!

THE NEED TO MEASURE

The need to measure and weigh things brought about one of the most important inventions of ancient peoples. They invented systems of measurement because they

The ancient Egyptians used standard measurements to help them in building and in dividing their fields.

105. TOMBE DE REKHMARA, CHEIKH ABD-EL-QOURNAH. PESÉE DE L'OR.

needed to know how big something was, or how much of something they had.

With standard units for length, a traveler could find out how far the journey to the next town was. An architect could tell the stonecutters exactly what size stones were

The Egyptians used standard measurements to plan their temples and pyramids.

needed to build the temple he designed. With standard units for weight, a woman would know how much milled wheat she could buy for one copper coin.

Without standard units of measurement, there was no way to communicate such information from one person to another.

Each civilization developed its own standard units. These were often similar because it was natural to use the

The world's oldest known dry measures. The small one holds one mouthful (80 cubic centimeters). The big one holds twice as much.

human body as a basis. For example, the unit of length we call a foot comes from old units that were based on the actual length of a man's foot. The word "mile" comes from *mille,* the Latin word for "thousand," since the ancient Roman mile equaled one thousand paces.

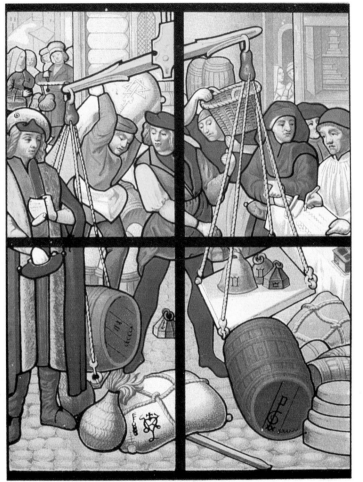

European merchants used
standard measures for the
bags and barrels of products
that they sold.

As the Roman Empire spread across the map, many parts of Europe adopted Roman measurements. Later, each European country developed its own system of weights and measures.

A certain stone kept in a marketplace might have been the standard unit of weight for merchants doing business there.

In Britain, to this day a person's weight is often given in "stones." (A stone equals 14 pounds, so if Reggie is 12 stone, he weighs 168 pounds–or, more properly in Britain, about 76 kilograms.)

In the 1600s, English settlers brought their measurement system to

In the United States, milk is usually sold in quarts, half-gallons, and gallons.

North America. And these
basic units of inches,
feet, and miles; ounces and
pounds; and pints, quarts,
and gallons are still used
in the United States.

ENTER METRIC

This French scale from the 1880s shows a person's weight in kilograms.

In 1670, a Frenchman named Gabriel Mouton said measurements should be based on the decimal system. Nothing happened, however, until the 1790s, when many people in France began to realize that a decimal-based system would be a help in science and trade.

By 1799, the essentials of a decimal-based system had been developed by the French Academy of Sciences. The name *metric* came from the ancient Greek word *metron,* meaning "a measure."

The system took some time to catch on. But eventually the French legislature passed a law requiring the use of the metric system in trade, beginning January 1, 1840.

In time, most other countries adopted the metric system, and its use in science quickly became universal. After Great Britain adopted the metric system in 1965, the United States was the only major country that had not officially gone metric.

Americans have been debating whether or not to go metric for about 150 years. Under the Constitution, Congress determines standards for weights and measures. An act of Congress in 1866 allowed people to use the metric system, but did not require it.

And in fact we do use the metric system a great deal. We may buy 35-millimeter film for a camera or a 2-liter bottle

We are used to buying camera film and soft drinks in metric sizes.

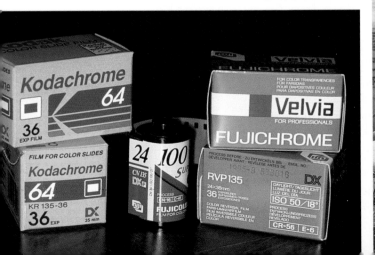

Track-and-field events are measured in metric units. These runners are competing in a 100-meter race. The electric meter in your home or apartment (inset) measures electricity in kilowatt-hours.

of soda. We pay a utility bill each month based on the number of kilowatt-hours of electricity we consume. A track-and-field meet may include a 100-meter dash. And all Olympic events, of course, are based on metric units of distance or weight.

Metric is going to show up more and more in your daily life—you can count on it. The only thing that hasn't been—and won't be—measured by the metric system is time. A minute is still 60 seconds and an hour is still 60 minutes. The seven-day week is also here to stay. And nothing can stop the Earth from taking 365 ¼ days to go around the sun.

MEET THE METER

The metric system starts with the meter, the basic unit of length. Just how long is a meter? Think of it as slightly longer than a yard, about 40 inches. So a basketball star might be two meters tall.

The French scientists who created the metric system had a rather complicated way of defining a meter. Consider an imaginary line, they said, on the Earth's surface, running from the equator through Paris to the North Pole. Then take one ten-millionth of this distance, and you have a meter.

Later on, the meter was officially determined as the distance between two lines

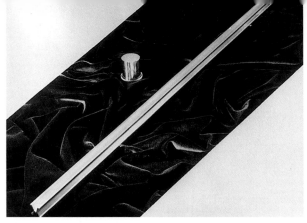

on a certain platinum-iridium bar. Similarly, a platinum-iridium weight was the standard kilogram. Both the bar and the weight are kept at the International Bureau of Weights and Measures in Sèvres, near Paris, France.

Today, scientists have a more exact way of defining a meter, accurate to one hundred-millionth of an inch!

METRIC UNITS

The basic metric units of weight, volume, and area are all based on the meter. A gram is the weight of the distilled water that would fill a cube one-hundredth of a meter along each edge (one cubic centimeter). A liter is the volume enclosed by a cube one-tenth of a meter along each edge. One liter of water weighs one kilogram, or one thousand grams.

The other units of measurement in the metric system are obtained by dividing or multiplying the basic units by 10, 100, 1,000, and so on. The prefix, or first part, of a unit's name increases or decreases the size of the unit. For example, *kilo* means "thousand," and a kilogram is 1,000 grams. *Centi* means "hundred,"

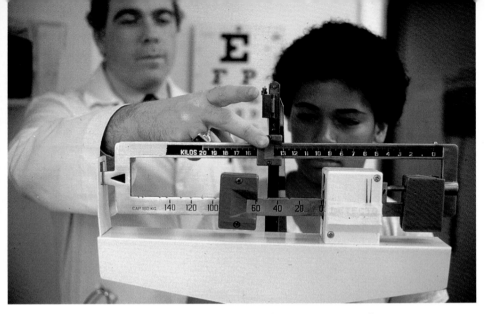

This scale shows both customary and metric measurements of weight.

and a centimeter is one-hundredth of a meter.

Table A lists these prefixes.

Table A: METRIC PREFIXES

Here are the prefixes for *divisions* of the basic units:

```
 deci = 0.1 (one-tenth)
centi = 0.01 (one-hundredth)
 milli = 0.001 (one-thousandth)
micro = 0.000001 (one-millionth)
```

These prefixes are used for *multiples* of the basic units:

```
 deka = times 10
hecto = times 100
 kilo = times 1000
mega = times 1,000,000
```

Table B: METRIC EQUIVALENTS

Units of Length

Millimeter	= 0.039 inch
Centimeter (10 millimeters)	= 0.39 inch
Meter (100 centimeters)	= 39.37 inches
Kilometer (1,000 meters)	= 0.62 mile

Units of Area

Square meter	= 10.76 square feet
Are (100 square meters)	= 1,076 square feet
Hectare (100 ares)	= 2.47 acres

Units of Weight

Gram	= 0.035 ounce
Kilogram (1,000 grams)	= 2.2 pounds
Metric ton (1,000 kilograms)	= 1.1 tons

Units of Capacity (Liquid Measure)

Deciliter	= 0.21 pint
Liter (10 deciliters)	= 1.06 quarts
Dekaliter (10 liters)	= 2.64 gallons

In Table B, "Metric Equivalents," the most commonly used metric units are shown, along with their equivalents in the English, or customary, system.

There are many other metric units, from milligrams to kiloliters. Their prefixes tell you how they relate to the commonly used units listed in Table B.

A tool and die maker uses a metric measure to judge the accuracy of a part he is making.

Table C, "Common Equivalents," lists some of the standard measures you're used to, and their approximate equivalents in metric units.

Table C: COMMON EQUIVALENTS

1 inch	=	2.5 centimeters
1 foot	=	30 centimeters
1 yard	=	0.9 meter
1 mile	=	1.6 kilometers
1 acre	=	0.4 hectare
1 ounce	=	28 grams
1 pound	=	0.45 kilogram
1 ton	=	0.9 metric ton
1 pint	=	0.47 liter
1 quart	=	0.95 liter
1 gallon	=	3.8 liters

This measuring cup is marked with both metric and customary units.

THE CELSIUS SCALE

The metric temperature scale is called the Celsius scale.

On a Celsius thermometer, the freezing point of water is 0 degrees and the boiling point of water is 100 degrees.

These thermometers show the temperature in degrees Celsius.

On a Fahrenheit thermometer, the freezing point of water is 32 degrees and the boiling point of water is 212 degrees.

There are 100 degrees from freezing to boiling on the Celsius scale. But from freezing to boiling on the Fahrenheit scale is 180 degrees (212–32). So each Celsius degree is equal to 1.8 Fahrenheit degrees.

This outdoor thermometer has both Fahrenheit and Celsius scales. The temperature is 26 degrees Fahrenheit–almost 4 degrees below zero Celsius.

To convert Fahrenheit to Celsius, subtract 32 from the Fahrenheit temperature and then multiply by $\frac{5}{9}$. For example, if your Fahrenheit thermometer reads 61 degrees, you subtract 32 from 61 and get 29, then multiply:

$$\frac{29}{1} \times \frac{5}{9} = \frac{145}{9} = 16\frac{1}{9}$$

or approximately 16 degrees Celsius.

Since most of us have trouble doing fractions quickly—or even slowly—in our heads, there's a simple shortcut we can use. To change Fahrenheit to Celsius, just subtract 30 from the Fahrenheit number and divide by 2. To go from Celsius to Fahrenheit, double the Celsius number and add 30. The results are not exact, but they are close enough so that you'll know whether you need a coat!

Pablo Morales of California won the 100-meter butterfly swimming race at the 1992 Olympic Games.

THINK METRIC

Of course you don't want to keep "translating" back and forth between metric and the customary system. It's much better to think directly in metric terms. When you read about a 100-meter swimming race in the Olympic Games, picture a pool 100 meters long.

Try measuring your long walks in kilometers instead of miles. (If it takes 20 minutes to walk a mile, you will walk a kilometer in about 12 ½ minutes.) Learn how heavy a kilogram feels, then practice judging how much familiar objects weigh directly in kilograms. Each morning, estimate the outside temperature in Celsius, without converting from Fahrenheit.

With a little practice, it's easy to learn to "think metric."

It won't be long before you've mastered the simpler, more logical metric system. And once you're thinking metric, you'll be in sync with the rest of the world.

WORDS YOU SHOULD KNOW

approximate (uh • PRAHK • sih • mit)–close; more or less exact

architect (AR • kih • tekt)–a person who designs houses and other buildings

Celsius (SEL • see • uss)–a temperature scale in which the freezing point of water is 0 degrees and the boiling point of water is 100 degrees

centimeter (SEN • tih • mee • ter)–one-hundredth of a meter in the metric system of measurement

civilization (siv • ih • lih • ZAY • shun)–a nation that has reached an advanced stage of development, with arts, sciences, and government

complicated (KAHM • plih • kay • tid)–hard to understand; not simple or easy

customary (KUSS • tuh • mair • ee)–the usual way of doing something

decimal (DESS • ih • mil)–based on the number ten

distilled (diss • TILD)–evaporated and then condensed; distilled water is free of most impurities

equator (ih • KWAY • ter)–an imaginary line around the earth, equally distant from the North and South poles

equivalent (e • KWIV • uh • lint)–something that is equal to or the same as another thing

essentials (eh • SEN • shilz)–necessary things; requirements

eventually (eh • VEN • chuh • lee)–finally; after a while

Fahrenheit (FAIR • in • hyt)–a temperature scale in which the freezing point of water is 32 degrees and the boiling point of water is 212 degrees

imaginary (ih • MAJ • in • air • ee)–made up; not real

kilogram (KIL • oh • gram)–a metric unit of weight, equal to 1,000 grams

kiloliter (KIL • oh • lee • ter)–a metric unit of volume, equal to 1,000 liters

kilometer (kil • AHM • ih • ter)–a metric unit of length, equal to 1,000 meters

kilowatt-hour (KIL • oh • watt OWR)–a unit that measures electrical energy

liter (LEE • ter)–a metric unit of capacity, equal to 1 cubic decimeter

logical (LAHJ • ik • il)–based on logic or reason

meter (MEE • ter)–the basic unit of measurement in the metric system

milligram (MIL • ih • gram)–a metric unit of weight, equal to one-thousandth of a gram

platinum-iridium (PLAT • ih • num eh • RID • ee • yum)–made of the two elements platinum, a white precious metal, and iridium, a hard silver-colored metal

prefix (PREE • fix)–a group of letters joined to the beginning of a word to change its meaning

random (RAN • dum)–done by chance, without order or planning

standard (STAN • derd)–accepted as a rule or model

technical (TEK • nih • kil)–having to do with industrial arts or skills

translating (tranz • LAY • ting)–putting into the words of another language

universal (yoo • nih • VER • sil)–used by people all over the world

INDEX

About the Author

*Allan Fowler is a free-lance writer with a background in advertising.
Born in New York, he lives in Chicago now and enjoys traveling.*